CLEOPATRA

BOUDICA

ZENOBIA

WU ZETIAN

ELEANOR

RAZIA

JADWIGA

NONHELEMA

GRACE O'MALLEY

Meet your FABULOUSLY FEISTY QUEENS!

You might think all queens do the same things: hand out medals, eat off gold plates, wave a lot and so on. Not these queens! Whether they ruled 2,000 years ago or last year – or whether they're called by a different title, such as chieftess or empress – each made a difference to their lands and their people. But, as you'll see, not in the same way. Take a look – they're fabulous!

NOOR

ELIZABETH II

WILHELMINA

YAA ASANTEWAA

CATHERINE THE GREAT

ELIZABETH I

CLEOPATRA

QUEEN OF EGYPT

c. 69–30 BCE

FAMED FOR HER BEAUTY, CLEOPATRA WAS CERTAINLY PRETTY... PRETTY AWESOME AT BEING THE STRONGEST AND CLEVEREST QUEEN THAT EGYPT HAS EVER KNOWN!

Cleopatra was very brainy and studied hard. She spoke several languages and was a brilliant student of history and medicine.

Strong, clever and famous... Cleopatra is PURRFECT.

WORLD HISTORY

FEMALE POWER

MODERN MEDICINE

DICTIONARY

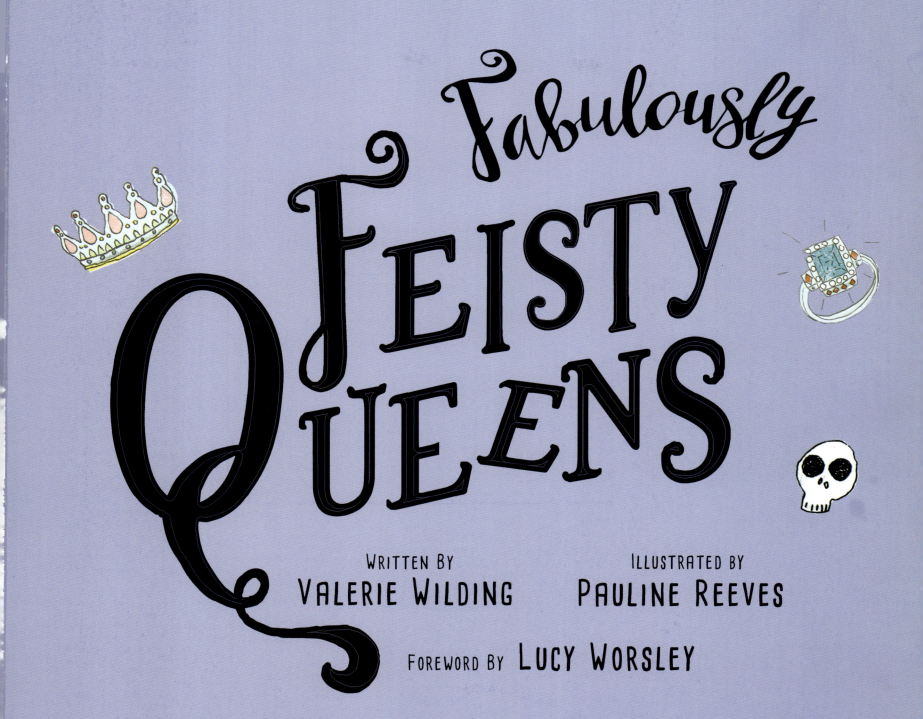

Fabulously FEISTY QUEENS

WRITTEN BY
Valerie Wilding

ILLUSTRATED BY
Pauline Reeves

FOREWORD BY Lucy Worsley

wren
&rook

A FOREWORD BY LUCY WORSLEY

Would you like to be a QUEEN? If you'd asked me that question before I began reading this book, I'd have said, "Nah, don't think I would, thank you."

The thing people don't always realise is that being a queen can be quite BORING. If you're a queen, you have to live by the rules of royal life, which are pretty strict. You have to wear the clothes other people want you to wear. You often have to marry a person you don't particularly want to marry. And your diary's so full of all your royal duties that you don't have time to travel into space, or make a scientific discovery, or write a novel. You're just too busy polishing your JEWELS or plotting against your ENEMIES.

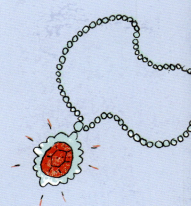

As I worked my way through the queens in this book, though, I started to notice that 'boring' isn't really the right word for their lives.

Terrifying, maybe. Courageous, maybe. But never dull. Queen Elizabeth I, for example, had to spend time in prison before she got to her throne. The Pirate Queen Grace O'Malley (I love her) wasn't born with her power – she made it for herself, through her ferocious actions. And then Catherine the Great got her power by stealing it from her useless husband. These people don't sound like they followed the usual royal rules.

And I realised that the queens who've made it into this book aren't here just because they were queens.

They're here because they were FEISTY and FABULOUS. That's the important bit. It's highly unlikely that you'll be a queen when you grow up (and I'm not sure you'd enjoy it anyway) but this is a GOOD THING. You'll have more time to become an astronaut, or a novelist, or maybe even an historian like me. In fact, it doesn't really matter what it is you do, just as long as you're fabulously feisty while you're doing it.

Happy reading!

CLEOPATRA was only 18 when she was made queen of Egypt. She knew that the greedy Romans wanted to conquer Egypt because it was a rich land – but Cleopatra wasn't about to let that happen!

Legend has it that when Caesar visited Egypt, a carpet was unrolled in front of him and **OUT POPPED** Cleopatra!

When Julius Caesar, a powerful Roman leader, visited Egypt, Cleopatra reasoned that if he fell in love with her, he would help her protect Egypt from the Romans. So she went on a mission to charm Caesar – and it worked. He was crazy about her! But it wasn't long before the rowdy Romans saw that Caesar was getting too **POWERFUL** and one day they murdered him…

When Cleopatra met Antony, she dressed as a goddess on a fabulous golden barge with purple sails. Clouds of perfume filled the air around her.

Cleopatra was sad but time passed and she then fell in love with Mark Antony. And when a high-powered Roman called Octavian declared **WAR** on Egypt, Cleopatra went into battle alongside her new husband.

She fought bravely, but when Octavian looked sure to win, she raced home to defend her precious Egypt. Antony escaped the battle and followed her. But back in Egypt, he heard rumours that Cleopatra was dead and threw himself on his sword. Cleopatra was heartbroken and shortly after is thought to have died from a snake bite. What a tragic end for such a **COURAGEOUS** queen!

Boudica
Queen of the Iceni
c. 30 – c. 60 CE

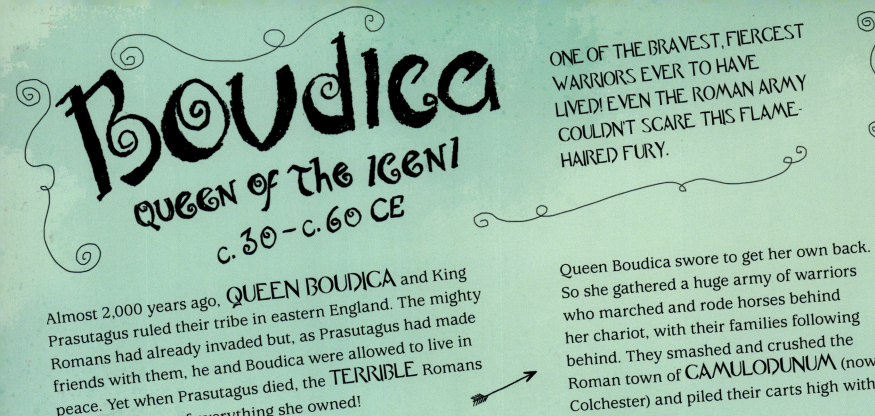

ONE OF THE BRAVEST, FIERCEST WARRIORS EVER TO HAVE LIVED! EVEN THE ROMAN ARMY COULDN'T SCARE THIS FLAME-HAIRED FURY.

Almost 2,000 years ago, QUEEN BOUDICA and King Prasutagus ruled their tribe in eastern England. The mighty Romans had already invaded but, as Prasutagus had made friends with them, he and Boudica were allowed to live in peace. Yet when Prasutagus died, the TERRIBLE Romans robbed Boudica of everything she owned!

Queen Boudica swore to get her own back. So she gathered a huge army of warriors who marched and rode horses behind her chariot, with their families following behind. They smashed and crushed the Roman town of CAMULODUNUM (now Colchester) and piled their carts high with stolen goodies.

CAMULODUNUM

LONDINIUM

Then they stormed through the biggest Roman town, LONDINIUM (now London). They trashed it and burned whatever was left.

Boudica's warriors loved scaring their enemies. Before battle they painted their bodies with blue dye. Some spiked their hair and stripped off completely.

ZENOBIA

C. 240–274

QUEEN OF PALMYRA

THE DESERT QUEEN WITH THE HEART OF A LION!

I'm totally the **greatest** queen ever!

QUEEN ZENOBIA lived with King Odaenathus in beautiful Palmyra. This was a rich city in a Syrian oasis where rustling palm trees shaded people's homes from the desert sun. Many lands around Palmyra belonged to the Romans, but their armies were friendly with the king and queen, and left the city alone.

Yet when Zenobia's son was still young, the king died. Someone had to take charge and RULE Palmyra until the boy grew up. Who else but Queen Zenobia?

The FEARLESS and FEISTY queen wanted to make Palmyra greater than ever, so she wasn't friends with the Romans any more. She galloped into battle and declared herself queen of every land and city she captured.

BRAVE Zenobia invaded Egypt, battled against the Roman army — and won! The emperor was livid, especially as Rome got lots of its food from Egypt.

Grrr!
Look at her parading around with all her silks and jewels — who does she think she is? The queen?

Then the next Roman emperor sent an army to ATTACK Palmyra and get Egypt back. Zenobia fought bravely, but the Roman army was huge, and too strong for her warriors. Zenobia escaped, but the Romans caught her and made her walk in the Emperor's great victory parade.

Zenobia wasn't allowed to return to Palmyra. Yet the Romans respected this FEISTY queen and it's said they let her live in style in a big villa near their city, Rome!

9

WU ZETIAN

EMPRESS OF CHINA   624–705

THE TOUGH CHINESE EMPRESS WHO LET NO ONE STAND IN HER WAY!

WU ZETIAN was young and clever. Emperor Gaozong of China fell in love with her. But Gaozong became ill, so Zetian took over his work duties. And she loved it!

When Gaozong died, their son was made emperor, but he wouldn't do as Zetian wanted so she sent him away. She knew she could do the job better. Zetian announced that she was the **EMPRESS** and got rid of anyone who said otherwise!

China grew **STRONG** and rich under its first (and last) female emperor.

In Wu Zetian's time, not many girls could read and write. Zetian's father made sure she was educated – that's why she was able to step in and take charge.

I'm not as good as a man. I'm BETTER!

WOW! The empress is doing a man's job – and doing it BRILLIANTLY!

When Zetian was empress, anyone who said a woman couldn't rule was banished.

I was 15 when I married King Louis VII and became queen of France. But I wasn't happy. "I don't want to be with you any more," I said, some years later. "Let's split up." Louis refused at first, but in the end he changed his mind. I was freeee!

I married Henry of Anjou soon after. When he became Henry II, king of England, I was queen again! It was a lively marriage, with lots of children and lots of squabbles!

Eventually, I was totes fed up with Henry (too many girlfriends!). "I'm not hanging about here," I thought, so I went home to Aquitaine. I was still the duchess there, and I ruled alone.

ELEANOR OF AQUITAINE

QUEEN OF FRANCE AND ENGLAND
DUCHESS OF AQUITAINE

C.1122–1204

MARRIED TO TWO KINGS, MOTHER OF TWO MORE, THIS POWERFUL QUEEN DIDN'T LET ANYTHING GET HER DOWN – ESPECIALLY A RUBBISH HUSBAND!

Five years later I almost got my own back on Henry. Three of our sons tried to force him off the throne. Did I support them? You bet! But it all went wrong, and cruel Henry kept me prisoner in one dismal castle after another. For years!

Now Henry's dead and my darling son Richard is KING OF ENGLAND! He's going to set me FREE!

The End
(for now)

Here we go again. Where to this time?

After Richard freed ELEANOR he went off to war, leaving her in charge. And then tragedy struck! Richard died and his unpopular brother, John, became king. But Eleanor, now in her seventies, worked hard to support King John.

When she last set out to help him in battle, she was 80. What an AMAZING royal career!

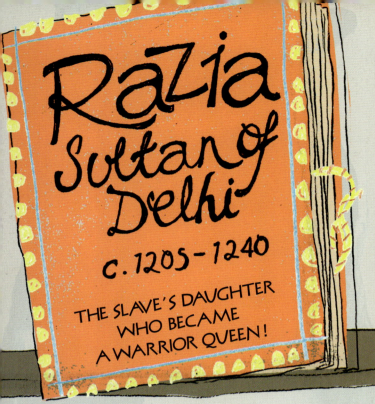

Razia Sultan of Delhi

c. 1205 – 1240

THE SLAVE'S DAUGHTER WHO BECAME A WARRIOR QUEEN!

RAZIA was the first and last female sultan of Delhi in India. She ruled for only four years, but in that time she set up schools and libraries, and led her warriors into battle. Razia wanted to make her kingdom LARGER and STRONGER. She proved that a woman could lead her people as well as any man.

Marry my daughter and when I die you will become Sultan.

Razia's father was a slave who became an important officer. His owner, the old sultan, set him FREE.

Princess Razia learned to FIGHT, riding horses and elephants and, when her father became the new sultan, she learned how to rule by watching him.

My brothers just fool around, learning nothing. Useless lot.

The sultan wondered who would rule after him.

Razia's smarter than her brothers. I want her to be sultan after me, but will the people like a woman ruler?

When Razia's father died, she knew she must be strong, so the people would TRUST her to look after them.

A female sultan should be called sultana. But I'm as good as any man. I am Razia Sultan.

Men who HATED the idea of a woman ruler went to war against her. Their leader was called Altunia.

Razia was once my friend, but if the people don't want her as sultan, I must do as they wish!

I don't believe it! Altunia's turned against me!

JADWIGA

c.1373–1399

THE HUNGARIAN-BORN PRINCESS WHO BECAME THE KING OF POLAND, AGED 11!

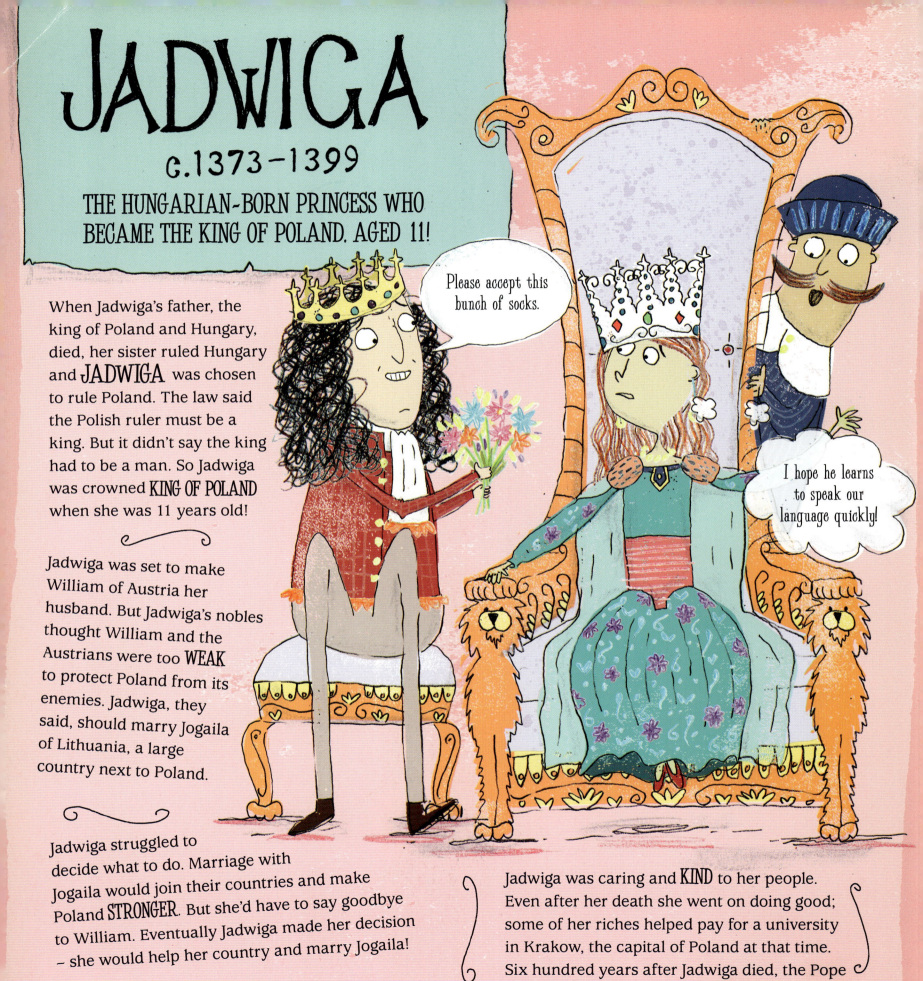

When Jadwiga's father, the king of Poland and Hungary, died, her sister ruled Hungary and JADWIGA was chosen to rule Poland. The law said the Polish ruler must be a king. But it didn't say the king had to be a man. So Jadwiga was crowned KING OF POLAND when she was 11 years old!

Jadwiga was set to make William of Austria her husband. But Jadwiga's nobles thought William and the Austrians were too WEAK to protect Poland from its enemies. Jadwiga, they said, should marry Jogaila of Lithuania, a large country next to Poland.

Jadwiga struggled to decide what to do. Marriage with Jogaila would join their countries and make Poland STRONGER. But she'd have to say goodbye to William. Eventually Jadwiga made her decision – she would help her country and marry Jogaila!

Jadwiga was caring and KIND to her people. Even after her death she went on doing good; some of her riches helped pay for a university in Krakow, the capital of Poland at that time. Six hundred years after Jadwiga died, the Pope made her a saint.

CHIEF NONHELEMA of the Shawnee tribe was a fearsome warrior in America. But she and her brother, Chief Cornstalk, agreed peace between their tribe and the people who had come to settle in their homeland.

When Britain went to **WAR** with the settlers in 1775, the Shawnee sided with the British. But even though it angered her people, Nonhelema stuck passionately to her promise of **PEACE**.

NONHELEMA

c.1720–1786

THE NATIVE AMERICAN CHIEFTESS WHOSE NAME MEANS 'NOT A MAN'!

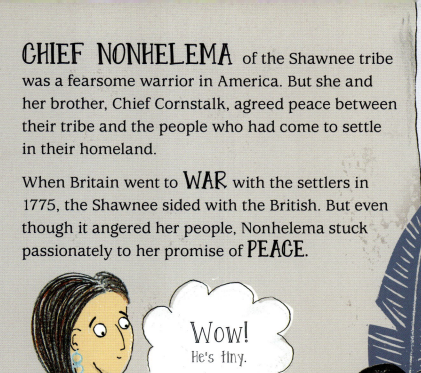

Wow! He's tiny.

Gosh! She's tall.

Nonhelema was nicknamed *The Grenadier Squaw* because she was as tall as a Grenadier guard. Grenadiers were British soldiers known for their height. Nonhelema was nearly six feet six inches tall!

MY MISSIONS

MISSION ONE

I must warn the Americans in Fort Randolph that my Shawnee people have sided with the British (the fools!) and are about to attack.

MISSION TWO

I have to get my brother, Cornstalk, to stop his warriors from attacking the Americans!

MISSION TWO UPDATE

Cornstalk failed and was killed. But that won't stop me working for peace. I speak Shawnee and English. I'll be an interpreter. Talking is better than fighting!

MISSION THREE

A year has passed since Cornstalk died and we are still at war. Today I'll disguise two soldiers as tribesmen, so the Shawnee will let them pass. They can gallop to Fort Donnally to warn the Americans that they're about to be attacked.

MISSION UPDATE

The war's been over for three years, and my people call me a traitor for helping the Americans. But I won't be put off – maybe I'll help make a Shawnee dictionary so, in future, the two sides will be able to talk. I'll never stop believing in peace and that I did the right thing.

GRACE O'MALLEY
PIRATE QUEEN   c. 1530–1603

THE FIERCE AND FEARSOME IRISH PIRATE WHO DARED TO CHALLENGE THE QUEEN OF ENGLAND.

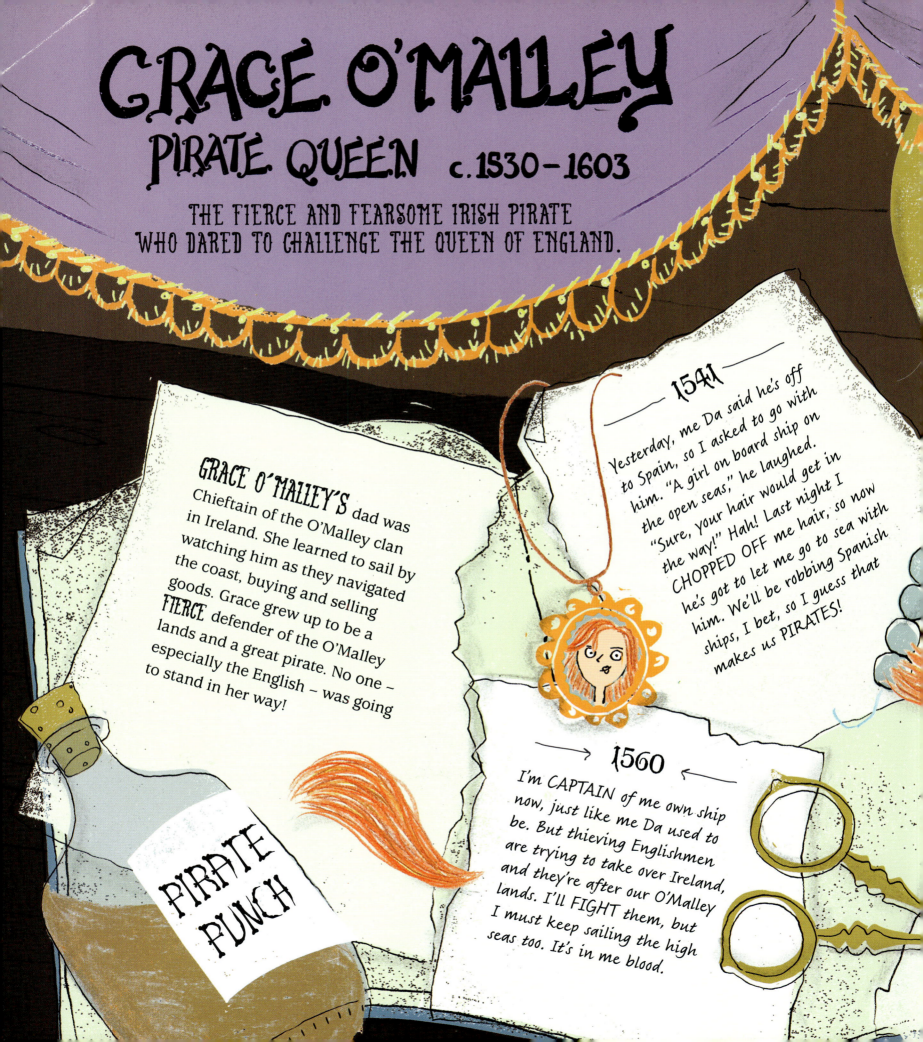

GRACE O'MALLEY'S dad was Chieftain of the O'Malley clan in Ireland. She learned to sail by watching him as they navigated the coast, buying and selling goods. Grace grew up to be a **FIERCE** defender of the O'Malley lands and a great pirate. No one – especially the English – was going to stand in her way!

PIRATE PUNCH

1541
Yesterday, me Da said he's off to Spain, so I asked to go with him. "A girl on board ship on the open seas," he laughed. "Sure, your hair would get in the way!" Hah! Last night I CHOPPED OFF me hair, so now he's got to let me go to sea with him. We'll be robbing Spanish ships, I bet, so I guess that makes us PIRATES!

1560
I'm CAPTAIN of me own ship now, just like me Da used to be. But thieving Englishmen are trying to take over Ireland, and they're after our O'Malley lands. I'll FIGHT them, but I must keep sailing the high seas too. It's in me blood.

Give me your gold, you SCURVY seadogs - and your pirate punch!

— 1579 —
Me and my brave crew have ROBBED loads of pirate ships, and English ones too. I'm rich! Rich! I'm the Pirate Queen!

— 1593 —
I've had enough of BATTLING to keep the English away. I'm off to tell their queen that no scabby Englishman's stealing O'Malley lands!

→ 1593 ←
I've been to Queen Elizabeth's great palace in England! To be sure, we got on fine. She said I can keep me lands, and I promised not to ATTACK her English ships.

ELIZABETH I

Queen of England and Ireland 1533-1603

ELIZABETH'S REIGN IS KNOWN AS A GOLDEN AGE OF MUSIC, LITERATURE, EXPLORATION — AND SOME REALLY EXCELLENT THEATRE!

Elizabeth loved her food. Unfortunately, she loved sugar a little too much...

I wonder why all my teeth are black?

Over 450 years ago, ELIZABETH I was crowned queen. Many people thought a woman couldn't be a good monarch, but Elizabeth believed in herself. She resolved to prove that she was as capable as any king.

Elizabeth ruled for 44 years and the people adored and RESPECTED her. She kept her country safe in times of war, and she made it powerful. She was one of Britain's greatest monarchs ever!

Elizabeth's father was Henry VIII and her mother was his second queen, Anne Boleyn. Henry had six wives altogether. Four of them became Elizabeth's stepmothers, though none of them were around for long.

I've heard of multitasking, but that's ridiculous!

Young Elizabeth was extremely clever. She had an amazing memory and learned French, Latin, Italian, Spanish and Greek while she was still a child.

Elizabeth loved music, dancing, poetry and art. People like William Shakespeare put on plays in her palaces, and that made them famous. It made theatres popular too.

When Elizabeth's long, red hair grew thin and grey, she wore magnificent wigs so people wouldn't think she was getting too old and frail to rule.

When Elizabeth was a princess, she was sent to the Tower of London as a prisoner by her half-sister, Queen Mary. Mary had once been kind, but she was scared stiff that Elizabeth's followers might want to get rid of her and make Elizabeth queen. Elizabeth spent nine frightening weeks in prison, wondering what would happen to her.

Elizabeth mounted a white horse and made an inspiring speech to her sailors before they went to fight the Spanish. To show that she was as powerful as any king, she wore a silver helmet and shining body armour over her white velvet gown.

Catherine The Great
Empress Of Russia 1729–1796

THE GERMAN PRINCESS WHO MADE A MIGHTY EMPIRE EVEN MIGHTIER!

Sixteen-year-old Princess Sophie of Germany was married to a young half-Russian man called Peter. His aunt was the empress of Russia and when she died, Peter became emperor. Sophie learned to speak Russian, and even took a Russian name: Yekaterina. We know her as *CATHERINE THE GREAT*.

Catherine thought her husband was a pretty useless *EMPEROR*. So did lots of other people, including his army.

Peter was *ARRESTED* and died, so Catherine was quickly crowned Empress.

She worked so hard to make Russia a better place to live that the Russians loved her and called her Little Mother. But Catherine did far more than care for her people. In her 34-year reign, she made the Russian empire larger, richer and *STRONGER*. That's why she's remembered as *CATHERINE THE GREAT!*

TO DO
- OPen college
- open Hospital
- start new girls' school
- Try vaccine

YAA ASANTEWAA was Queen Mother of part of the Asante empire, in what is now Ghana, Africa. Some Queen Mothers were mothers of kings or queens, but Yaa Asantewaa was given the title by her brother, who was chief of another district.

YAA ASANTEWAA

c.1830s – 1921

THE COURAGEOUS AFRICAN QUEEN AND HER GOLDEN STOOL.

The British wanted to **CONTROL** the Asante people, so the governor banished their king to the Seychelles. He also ordered the Asante people to give him their most precious object, the Golden Stool. This was the throne of the Asante people and Yaa Asantewaa was furious that the British wanted to sit on it!

Yaa Asantewaa and other Asante leaders met to decide how to rescue the king and **PROTECT** the stool. But Yaa Asantewaa was shocked to find that most of them were afraid of attacking the British. She was too proud to give in, so she announced that if the men wouldn't fight, the women would!

The Golden Stool holds our nation's soul. No foreigner will ever sit upon it!

The Asante rulers asked Yaa Asantewaa to **LEAD** an army of thousands against the British.

The British were too well-armed. They **WON** the war and also banished Yaa Asantewaa to the Seychelles.

She never returned home, but she's still remembered as a great **HEROINE**. This queen, who couldn't read or write, inspires young Ghanaian girls to this day!

WILHELMINA
1880–1962

THE DUTCH QUEEN WHOSE WARTIME RADIO MESSAGES INSPIRED HER PEOPLE!

Telegram NO.

16 MAY 40

AM SAFE. TO ENGLAND BY WARSHIP. TRAIN TO LONDON (IT WAS LATE). KING GEORGE TOOK US TO BUCKINGHAM PALACE.

WILHELMINA was ten when she became queen of the Netherlands. Her country didn't take sides in the First World War, but things were different in the Second World War. When the Germans invaded, she escaped to Britain with her family and some of her government ministers.

Throughout the war, Wilhelmina spoke to the Dutch people regularly on Radio Orange to keep their spirits up. When her prime minister decided it would be best to make peace with Hitler, Queen Wilhelmina said NO! The prime minister got **FIRED**. The queen appointed a new prime minister who would help her keep the Netherlands strong while they were away.

We won't let Hitler win while Queen W is around!

Keep smiling, everyone. Our country will be free one day!

Some Dutch people formed resistance groups to **FIGHT** secretly against the Germans. They were inspired by the queen's broadcasts and used her photograph as a sign that they were members of the resistance.

Wilhelmina only gave up the **THRONE** when she became too ill to carry on. She reigned for nearly 58 years!

ELIZABETH II

Queen of Great Britain, Northern Ireland – and more!

b. 1926–

NO OTHER LIVING KING OR QUEEN HAS REIGNED LONGER THAN THIS HARD-WORKING BRITISH MONARCH!

When PRINCESS ELIZABETH's uncle decided not to be king any more, her father stepped up and became King George VI. Straight away, life changed for Elizabeth and her sister, Margaret.

Philip's such a dreamboat. I'm going to marry him, I am!

When Elizabeth was 13, she met a HANDSOME young prince named Philip. She'd forgotten seeing him at a wedding when she was 8, but she'd never forget this meeting! She liked him a lot.

This is Margaret when Mummy told her I'd be queen one day. How does she think I felt?!

It's so lovely to be like the other girls, just for a while.

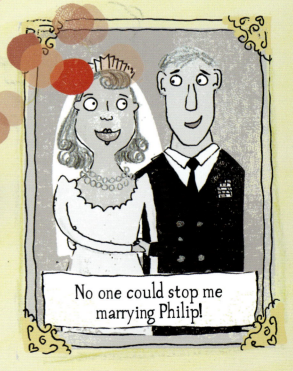

No one could stop me marrying Philip!

At the OUTBREAK of the Second World War, Philip went off to fight. Elizabeth joined the army and trained as a mechanic! She learned to drive, change wheels and fix engines.

Elizabeth and Philip wrote each other letters and he visited when he could. Some people thought he was wrong for her, but she was CRAZY about him and refused to give him up. After the war, she got her way.

Me on a walkabout, with rather a lot of flowers.

Just one of my many winners!

QUEEN SHOT AT **BY YOUTH**

Youth Marcus Sarjeant fired six blank shots at the Queen whose horse was startled. The Queen stayed calm and kept the horse under control.

Marcus Simon Sarjeant arrested for shooting blanks at the queen at the Trooping of the colour.

Once, Elizabeth — an ace horsewoman — was riding sidesaddle when someone FIRED blank shots at her. She showed no fear and simply rode on, controlling her horse beautifully.

A few years later, in 1952, Elizabeth's father died and she became QUEEN. From the day she was crowned, Elizabeth worked hard for her people, making official visits to other countries, launching ships, opening schools, making speeches and supporting charities.

Long ago, on Elizabeth's 21ST birthday, she promised to devote her life to her people. She kept that promise. Even when she reached 90, this strong, determined queen didn't stop working – or smiling!

NOOR

b.1951-

THE ECO-FRIENDLY QUEEN WHO WON'T BE A CHEERLEADER!

LISA HALABY was born and brought up in the USA. She swam, played sports, rode her Arabian horse and studied hard. One day, her father took her to a ceremony in the Kingdom of Jordan. When King Hussein appeared, Lisa's dad asked her to take his photo with the King.

The king and Lisa became friends and spent a lot of time together. One day, he PROPOSED. Lisa knew that if she married him, there would be huge changes in her life, and she took some weeks to decide. Her answer was, "Yes!"

Lisa tried cheerleading when she was a teenager. But she didn't like the tiny skirts and ankle socks so she decided to wear trousers instead.

Becoming queen of another country meant that Lisa had to learn a whole new language – Arabic. The king even gave her an Arabic name, which was Noor Al-Hussein. This means *'LIGHT OF HUSSEIN'*.

Queen Noor is passionate about getting rid of nuclear weapons. She cares for the environment too, and makes sure the royal family sets a good example. Noor even took three of her princesses and princes to city parks to pick up litter.

NO MORE NUCLEAR WEAPONS!

Noor became stepmother to the king's children and had four of her own. Busy as she was, she spent a lot of her time helping people and *SUPPORTING* charities, especially those that work for peace.

Noor is keen on improving life for women and young people; she helped to start Jordan's first children's hospital. Even after the king died, Noor carried on working.

QUEENS OF TOMORROW

A **PRINCESS** who is destined to become the next queen of a country is sometimes known as a crown princess. Some, like Sweden's Victoria, are the eldest children of kings and queens. Others might be princesses or ordinary women who marry crown princes. Young or not-so-young, they all have loads to learn and can make differences to lives around the world. Let's take a look at some queens-to-be...

Learning to be a princess is challenging, but here's a Christmas tip. If you ever have to give the queen a present, don't panic! Make her something. I made chutney!

CATHERINE
Duchess of Cambridge
b. 1982–

Could sport-loving Catherine Middleton ever have dreamed that by choosing a particular university, she'd one day become her country's queen? It was while studying in Scotland that Catherine met her student prince, William. He's destined for the British throne, but not just yet; his father, the Prince of Wales, is next in line. Following him will be Prince William, and when he becomes king, Catherine will be queen!

Most princesses have roses or ships named after them – my namesake is a polar research station in Antarctica!

PRINCESS ELISABETH
Duchess of Brabant
b. 2001–

Teenage Elisabeth will be the first Belgian queen to rule in her own right. She speaks French and German, and went to school in Brussels, where she was taught in Dutch. Her parents then sent her to boarding school in an ancient Welsh castle where she could learn English, and maybe some Welsh. When her time comes, she'll definitely be ready to rule!

MARY
Crown Princess of Denmark
b. 1972–

When Australian Mary Donaldson met a handsome Danish man in a pub in Sydney, he didn't tell her, at first, that one day he'd be king of Denmark. He'd gone to watch the Olympics and ended up with a girlfriend! Once they were married, Mary took part in all the usual activities of a princess. She also joined part of the army, the Danish Home Guard. She learned to shoot, march, fight fires and send signals, and reached the rank of first lieutenant. Princesses really can do anything!

CATHARINA-AMALIA
Princess of Orange
b. 2003–

Another teenager, Catharina-Amalia is a princess three times over: she's princess of Orange, princess of the Netherlands and princess of Orange-Nassau. What's important, though, is that she's destined to be queen of the Netherlands. Amalia isn't old enough yet for royal duties and her father, the king, is happy for her to live as normal a life as possible.

VICTORIA
Crown Princess of Sweden
b. 1977–

Victoria has packed in plenty of experiences before she becomes queen. She's travelled, learned new languages, worked in Sweden's embassy in the USA and she's even had army training! Victoria has plenty of royal engagements to keep her busy, as well as a husband and two lively children. Her daughter, Princess Estelle, will follow her mum to the throne one day.

GLOSSARY

banish – punish someone by sending them away from their homeland

barge – a large flat-bottomed boat

chieftain – the leader of a clan or tribe

clan – a group of families who are all related

corruption – when powerful people are dishonest or break the law to get more power or money

emperor or empress – a male or female ruler of an empire

empire – a group of countries with the same ruler

heir to the throne – a person who is next in line to become king or queen

monarch – a ruler, such as a king, queen, emperor or empress

nobles – titled people such as lords, dukes and earls, who are often powerful

nuclear weapons – deadly weapons that use nuclear energy to cause destruction over a huge area

oasis – area in a desert where there's water, and plants and trees can grow

ransom – a large payment that must be made before a kidnapped person will be set free

resistance groups – people who join together to fight against a powerful person or government by spying and destroying equipment or property

sultan – a Muslim ruler

For Elsie and Eddie with love – V.W.
For Louise, I couldn't have done it without you – P.R.

First published in Great Britain in 2020
by Wren & Rook

Text copyright © Valerie Wilding, 2020
Illustration copyright © Pauline Reeves, 2020

The right of Valerie Wilding and Pauline Reeves to be identified as author and illustrator respectively of this work has been asserted by them in accordance with the Copyright, Designs and Patents Act 1988.

All rights reserved.

Hardback ISBN: 978 1 5263 6190 5
Paperback ISBN: 978 1 5263 6192 9
E-book ISBN: 978 1 5263 6191 2
10 9 8 7 6 5 4 3 2 1

FSC MIX Paper from responsible sources FSC® C104740

Wren & Rook
An imprint of
Hachette Children's Group
Part of Hodder & Stoughton
Carmelite House
50 Victoria Embankment
London EC4Y 0DZ
An Hachette UK Company
www.hachette.co.uk
www.hachettechildrens.co.uk

Publishing Director: Debbie Foy
Senior Editor: Laura Horsley and Alice Horrocks
Art Director: Laura Hambleton

Printed in China

Every effort has been made to clear copyright. Should there be any inadvertent omission, please apply to the publisher for rectification.

The website addresses (URLs) included in this book were valid at the time of going to press. However, it is possible that contents or addresses may have changed since the publication of this book. No responsibility for any such changes can be accepted by either the author or the publisher.